A SEASON OF

SPACIOUSNESS

A SEASON OF SPACIOUSNESS

words to hold you
as you reclaim your breath
and expand your capacity

tiffany celeste frenette

Copyright © 2022 by Tiffany Celeste Frenette

All rights reserved. No part of this book may be reproduced or transmitted in any form whatsoever without written permission from the publisher.

To protect the privacy of certain individuals, all names and identifying details in the legacy stories have been changed. The rest of this book is a work of fiction. Any names, characters, businesses or places, events or incidents are fictitious. Any resemblance to actual persons, living or dead, or actual events is purely coincidental.

Pebble Byway Press

Toronto, Canada

Illustrations, layout and design by Tiffany Celeste Frenette

Photographs by Tiffany Celeste Frenette or released under Creative Commons Zero License.

To contact the author:

Visit celestefrenette.com

To see more of the author's work:
Visit IG @celestefrenette
FB @celestefrenette

Book cover designed by Tiffany Celeste Frenette

Trade Paperback ISBN: 978-1-7778634-0-1
E-book ISBN: 978-1-7778634-1-8

Manufactured in Canada

10 9 8 7 6 5 4 3 2 1
1st edition, November 2022

For Jaiden and Mirahbelle
brave and beautiful
breath of my prayers

may the voice of your souls
ever be louder than the noise of the world

there is space here for you

I REMEMBER

I REMEMBER

barefoot on the earth
pulses of love ascend
anchoring me
winding helixes around my spine
holding me
weaving peace into my heart
reminding me

                you belong here

I am weightless
inside the belly of my mother
I feel my sister
beside me
we share lifetimes
every day
we compose symphonies and write timeless classics
we dream freedom dreams and plant seeds of promise

light begins to flicker
untamed tides turn upon themselves
I wake to see
my sister is no longer here with me
I drift in the vastness
alone
for the first time
I learn what it is to live without her

I look out at the world
gaze into the expanse of the windswept clouds
the sun whispers melodies of remembering
and I feel her again
I carry her songs with me
love pressed them into the grooves of my heart
and it brought me here
to sing them

I REMEMBER

home is where we are
love is who we are

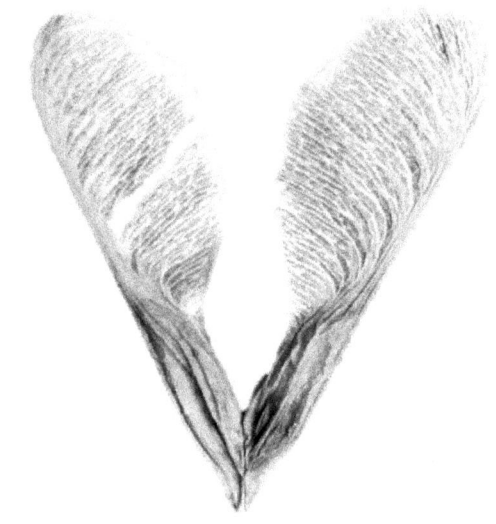

I REMEMBER

It's not going to be okay
but you will be

everything is going to fall apart,
more than once

you will endure losses
you didn't think you could bear

and it will ache
and you will cry
and you will want to give up

but you won't

because the life inside of you
will choose to keep living

and the broken pieces
will show you your wholeness

and the ache will teach you your strength
and the tears will water your dreams

and the life inside of you
will choose to keep living
and doing it all over again

It's not going to be okay
not always
but you will be

and so, this is life:

love brings me back to the truth of who I am

over and over and over again

I REMEMBER

she belongs
but she doesn't fit in

she belongs
like the sun belongs to the earth
and the stars belong to the sky
and our hearts belong to each other

in a world full of people living half alive
who forget who they are and why
she remembers

she belongs
but she doesn't fit in
and most days
she doesn't really want to

she remembers

in a world that forgets

THE

WORLD

HAS

BEEN

WAITING

FOR

YOU

ALL OF ITS LIFE

I REMEMBER

she found her truth there

buried deep under her desire

to make others happy

        so, she dug it out

                and put it on top

                        where it belonged

this is not a test

I REMEMBER

we are given opportunities to be who we are

not to prove who we are

the universe already knows us

it is only us who forget sometimes

breathe

you don't have to try so hard

more you

is what the world is missing

I REMEMBER

more you

looks good on you

I will be more me ♡

I REMEMBER

let's be honest

it's exhausting
wanting to be liked
editing yourself
walking on eggshells
treading the narrow and impossible path
to a false sense of acceptance
from people you
don't even actually like

today

someday

has

arrived

I REMEMBER

I do not owe you your ideas of me
give them to me and I will light a bonfire
to brighten a pathway
you will never see
as I travel to places
you will never visit

She stood with her back towards the sun.
It illuminated everything in front of her
and everything around her.
She knew it was there – she felt its warm embrace and
saw its brightness, but she couldn't turn to face it.
It overwhelmed her.
She didn't feel worthy of it.

She spent her life facing the other direction,
and never, until her final moments on earth
when tears streamed down her face
as she gazed into a glowing white light
that felt like home,
did she realize that all along
it was her reflection.

I REMEMBER

 think of the
 most beautiful thing
  you've ever seen
 and understand that
it is your reflection

when we cannot bear the weight of this world,
and we cannot find the love of our source –
when all we want to do is go home

let's look towards the sun together

A JOURNEY OF REMEMBERING

I embark on a journey to discover my soul's purpose. As the drumbeat begins, I close my eyes and find myself above the clouds. I meet the expanse. Clear crystal quartz surrounds me like a sacred forest – radiant, sparkling, magnificent. The ground is soft, a waterfall rushes nearby, and the air is filled with fresh moss; I breathe it in deeply. It blankets my heart in peace. Calm and curious, I walk to meet my spirit guide.

The road bends, and a majestic lion stands in front of me. Graceful. Strong. Wise. I feel small and out of place but also safe. I resist the idea that the lion is here for me. I expect a bird or a deer – something smaller. I stand in awe, quiet like a young child gazing in sheer wonder.

"Why would a lion come to me?" I ask myself as my mind swirls with uncertainty.

The lion says, "You are called to be a leader."

I shrink and step back. I tell him, "I can't be a leader."

He says it again, steady and clear: "You are called to be a leader."

He may as well be speaking an entirely different language - I cannot even begin to grasp his words or find truth in them.

Confused, I say, "I'm not a leader."

He roars in my face; my hair blows back as my doubts are silenced.

He says again, "You are called to be a leader."

I give up. I lean into surrender and ask, "How? How can I be a leader?"

He replies, "You are called to lead by **love**."

I REMEMBER

I take a big deep breath. Relief flows through my body.

"Oh!" I exclaim. "THAT I can do!"

I understand at that moment that to lead by love means to be more *me*, to allow my heart to guide me and to love people the way I always have. It isn't daunting or complicated; it is something I can do because I am already doing it.

The lion walks closer and invites me to climb up on his back. I walk around and nestle in as his soft fur cloaks me in warmth. I reach my arms around his neck and hug him as he begins to run. The wind flows through my hair as it moves with his fur, and the two of us become one. I embody his grace, confidence and strength. To be powerful, my heart tells me, is to be rooted in the truth of who you are and where you come from – pure **love**. I thank him and hug him one more time. I leap down from that crystal cavern in the sky, and my feet touch the earth.

I breathe, and I remember who I am.

we are powerful

when

we remember

who we are

I REMEMBER

we will stand

side by side

and witness

the courage

that pours out of us

like all the love

of our ancestors

that can no longer

be contained

I REMEMBER

Held by the earth
Lifted by the mountains
Lit by the sun

right now

there are people

and places

dreaming

of meeting you

praying

to meet you

because

you

are the most anticipated highlight of their story

you
♡

are the highlight

and I know this because

you are mine, too

I REMEMBER

I dance in the quiet space
where loss and longing meet
where the ache and the emptiness
bleed into the lines of time
creating a void, I never knew I needed
for a future, I did not dare to dream of
filled with people I haven't even met yet
who will become some of the greatest loves of my life

A Legacy of Love

♡

Harold

It was my first year as a registered nurse, and I was assigned to work with the gruffest, grumpiest man on the ward, Harold. He barked orders at us. No *please*, no *thank you*. No warmth, no kindness. None of the nurses wanted him as their patient, but I didn't mind.

Truth be known, I love a good challenge. The best way to get me to do something is to tell me that I can't. I think I signed up for nursing school because when I first mentioned it to my boyfriend, he spat out his food from laughing so hard. "You! Around blood?!" He had a point, and I hated that.

Harold was in the hospital with terminal cancer. His children were distant and rarely came to visit. I did a lot of night shifts back then. There's something different about nursing at night; it's hard to describe. It was quieter and more peaceful than the day shift, but there was also a kind of vulnerability and open heartedness that emerged at night. It was like you got a window into the soul of people, and for a brief time the world wasn't moving so fast that you missed it.

After I had done my work and tended to everyone and everything that needed tending to, I'd take my charts into Harold's room. "It's kind of boring out at the nursing station Harold. Mind if I park here to work on my charts?"

He nodded his head and grunted at me. "Do what you like," he said.

We didn't talk much at first, but he started to share stories with me as time went on. He used to be a professor. It sounded like his students were scared of him, but as he listed their accomplishments and successes, I could feel how much he loved them and how proud he was.

He was a strict dad with his kids. He never told them how much he cared and figured they should already know. His daughter, Rachel, didn't like to be around him, but his eyes beamed when he talked about her and her kids.

I REMEMBER

It went on this way for months as his condition worsened. He got weaker, and the conversations got shorter and quieter. He wasn't especially warm or kind to me or any other nurses, but his rough edges softened. I knew his final moments were coming soon. His family came to say goodbye and went on their way.

Harold was in and out of consciousness on his last day, and when my shift ended, I just couldn't leave. I didn't want him to be alone. I stayed at the hospital that night, got myself a tea, sat by his side and held his hand. We didn't talk. He couldn't tell me anymore stories. He squeezed my hand, and that said it all. I stayed with him until his last breath.

It's easy to see someone who seems to lack kindness, compassion or respect and dismiss them. Easy to want to be unkind too. Treat them the way they treat you. Avoid them completely. It's understandable, and we do need to have boundaries, especially when it's someone close to us. I understood why his daughter couldn't be there with him. As a nurse, it was easier. I could see someone's story without being a part of it. I could bear witness.

Over the years, I noticed that the harshness people gave out was often what they were filled with. They didn't really need more of it – what they needed more of was love. Working in palliative care, I often noticed a softening, a returning of someone back to who they were before life got to them, hurt them and caused them to put up a wall. As their bodies began to fade, their true selves started to shine more brightly.

Of course, we don't need to be dying to do that; we can remember and return right now. The truth is always there underneath it all.

If we have love within us to give, let's give it. What pours out of us is also what will fill us, and maybe, just maybe, it will start to fill the hearts of the ones around us, too.

you can't escape life without some broken pieces

they come from living

the question is

can we meet those broken pieces with love

I REMEMBER

she broke

and then

she looked down at all the shattered pieces

and finally saw what she was made of

It is so much easier

to shatter

than to spend your life

trying to hold

broken pieces

that do not belong together

I REMEMBER

What else will I allow to break today?

I REMEMBER

what if our work

isn't to keep it all from falling apart

but to allow it

to fall apart sooner

I'll meet you there
in the space where our hearts are healing
in the *I don't know* and *too soon to tell*
in the *I hope* and *maybe one day*
in the peace of the quiet breath in between
where everything is lost
and nothing is promised
but we are brave enough
to show up and try again

I start a new story now

because I can

Love is a steady
and ever-present light
in my life

I REMEMBER

I write the word

love

on a bottle of water
and with every sip I take I say,
"I receive love"
it is a practice
a way of remembering
that it is safe to let love in

love

is

in

the

details

when I speak love into myself

it

is

healing

I REMEMBER

she looked bravely
into the darkest corners
and found that love resided

even there

especially there

always
there

WHISPER
to me slowly
as I fall in love
with the
remembering

I REMEMBER

all of life is aching for you to come home to yourself
everything around you
is your soul seeking to be remembered
longing to be remembered
whispering
shouting
wailing
to be remembered

in the energy

of love

it is impossible

to feel separate

from the truth

of who you are

I

DISCERN

I DISCERN

her heart was tender

and soft and open and

she liked it that way

so

she protected it

dear heart,

no one can protect you

like you can protect you

I DISCERN

my
no
is
as
sacred
as
my
yes

a promise to myself:
I will take more time before responding
I will find a place to quiet my mind
knowing that my thoughts are less important
than how I feel in my body
knowing that even when it's only a feeling I have
E S P E C I A L L Y
when it's only a feeling
I can trust it

it's easy to mistake noise for wisdom
the world is noisy after all
and the loud people shout
as if to proclaim
WE ARE POWERFUL
AND YOU ARE NOT
to make us think
we need to be more like them

they believe their noise is wisdom
but your body tells you

it

is

just

noise

I DISCERN

I listen for the quietest voices in the rooms I am in
I lean into the wisdom of the ones who don't take up
all the space
the ones who don't feel entitled to it
they remind me
to lean into the quiet of my heart
for the wisdom inside of me
they refer me
back to myself
and I know their wisdom is true
because it dances with mine
instead of trampling it

stay close to the ones

who feel easy to be around

that ease is your body whispering

"I feel safe"

YOU

DESERVE

TO

FEEL

SAFE

I hold tightly to the handrail

stopping to catch my breath

at

each

step

I sit down halfway through

I don't think I will survive this

and I am right

my body tells me a story of death

of letting go and giving up

I think it is me who will die

I'm wrong

it is my life

I DISCERN

I can't go on
doesn't mean I can't go on
it means
I must go on differently now

I DISCERN

I don't know where this path will lead me

but I know

it

will

not

take

me

to

places

I've

already

been

knowing I'd get

more

of what I said yes to

I started choosing

differently

I DISCERN

I let go of everything that is not me

and everything that is not mine

I let go of other people's ideas of me

whether I think they are right or they are wrong

I let go of their expectations of me

I let go even of their hopes for me

and as I do

my capacity

rushes back

like air to lungs gasping for breath

and I am filled with life again

my heart

reaches towards

the

light ♥

I DISCERN

my soul

reaches towards

the

darkness ♡

the darkness will not be ignored

it calls me in to wholeness

it pulls

relentlessly

on the sleeves of my sorrow

saying

I am here
I matter

I am a part of you, too

dive into me

dear one

bring your light with you

let us weave it through the depths

together

let us unearth all the beauty

that aches to be known

love waits for you here

peace waits for you

truth

waits for you

thundering rains
shake the earth
messy
wild
unrestrained
showing us
how
to
heal

I DISCERN

look at all that you've been through so far

and still, here you are

they will tell you to get over it

they will glaze over your anger

say cheer up, be more grateful

as they sentence you to death

with their well-intentioned ignorance

I DISCERN

don't get over it

not today

be with it instead

it is there either way

meet it with love

with tenderness

and curiosity

shine a light on it

unearth the truth

and it will breathe life into your cells

because anger is holy

too

from the day he was born
my son has been teaching me
how to heal
he teaches me by showing me
I will not suppress my feelings
I will not hide who I really am
I will not swallow my truth
I will not live to be your light
I am my own

I DISCERN

do not turn away

from the pain or the grief

or the truth

or the spectrum of feelings and experiences

that we call being human

instead

lean in

listen

witness

uplift

and

illuminate it all

knowing that

the spectrum

is a sacred part

of wholeness

WHOLENESS

heals

me

I DISCERN

that's just what you do
will never
guide my life
again
I'm leaving it right here
with *suck it up*
and *get over it*
while I build a life with
my *full body yes*
and *that feels right*

A JOURNEY OF DISCERNMENT

I walk with curiosity into the deep forest and encounter a great brown grizzly bear who stands to greet me. He is here to show me what I need to know about boundaries. I feel a familiar fear rise within me, and this is the first message: to trust my body. To let my feelings and intuition guide me. My body will always show me the truth. When something feels off, I must trust that. When I feel unsettled or unsafe around someone, when I feel exhausted around them - all of these are messages to support me in asserting my boundaries and doing what I need to do to be the guardian of my energy. The bear teaches me that it is safer to trust my body than my mind, and so I must always take the time to focus my awareness inward. He tells me that bears can protect themselves more easily than humans because when they know something's not right, they don't stop to think about it; they act.

Think less, feel more. You are the authority in your own life. It is safe to trust yourself.

An eagle swoops down, and my arms quickly reach up to grasp him. The two of us swirl through the air in a blissful dance of connection as we merge and become one. I feel the swiftness of his movements as he teaches me to act immediately and conserve the time and energy I often devote to indecision. I see a mouse on the ground and experience the peak precision of the eagle as we dive down, and he uses his claws to draw a line in the sand just millimeters away from that mouse. He tells me to be clear with my boundaries, draw a line in the sand, and be uncompromising when protecting my heart and soul. My feet touch the ground, and I stand there, integrating.

My ancestors stand in a circle behind me; they lay their hands on my back and remind me – I am supported and loved. Having healthy and firm boundaries in this life is safe and necessary.

The drum beat calls me back, and I thank the bear, the eagle and all my ancestors as I walk out of the forest with a renewed sense of strength and clarity.

my body doesn't lie

its every whisper is wisdom

I DISCERN

no creates space for yes

yes
to feeling good in my body

yes
to more time with my family

yes
to rest

yes
to joy

yes
to spaciousness

yes
to the freedom to choose

yes
even if it disappoints the people I love

yes

I'm going to trade in
imagining what might go wrong
for imagining
what might go right

this time

I will not rush to fill the emptiness

I will not look away from the void

I will dwell in the space in between

and breathe deeply into the unknown

as a silent, loving and sacred rebellion

I DISCERN

uncomfortable

and

beautiful

aching

and

peaceful

sad

and

trusting

all of it at the same time

there is space for it all

I had to let go
of hope

it sounds contrary
I know

we don't let go of hope
we expand it
we wrap the strings of longing around it
we carry it to meet our last breath if we must

that's what we have been taught

no matter what it takes
never give up

because hope will keep us going

but what if
we will die trying to hold it

what if letting go of the life we hoped for
is the one thing that will free us to the life that's waiting?

today
I notice
the places
and people
that make
breathing
easier

there is space here

for you

I will hold you

in the light of immense tenderness

wrap you

in the arms of love and compassion

and you

just

breathe

I DISCERN

let go of the love that doesn't know how to hold you

still, some days I need to remind myself:
the sun will rise tomorrow
and it will shine through the leaves for another day
there is beauty waiting
and it's worth staying for

I DISCERN

               for today
                 I trust
         that my path is my path
           even if no one else
             understands it

I feel the weight of loss on my chest

in a plea to the heavens, I cry

I just want to go home

love meets me there

with a deep breath of grace

my soul whispers

you are home, you're just

experiencing it differently

I speak love into my body
I speak peace into my heart
I speak healing into my cells
and so it is
and so it is
and so it is

I DISCERN

she called back
every single piece of herself
she had given away
and declared
herself
W H O L E

the truer I am to myself

the simpler life becomes

not easier

but simpler

I DISCERN

complexity and overwhelm
expand when I resist
my inner knowing

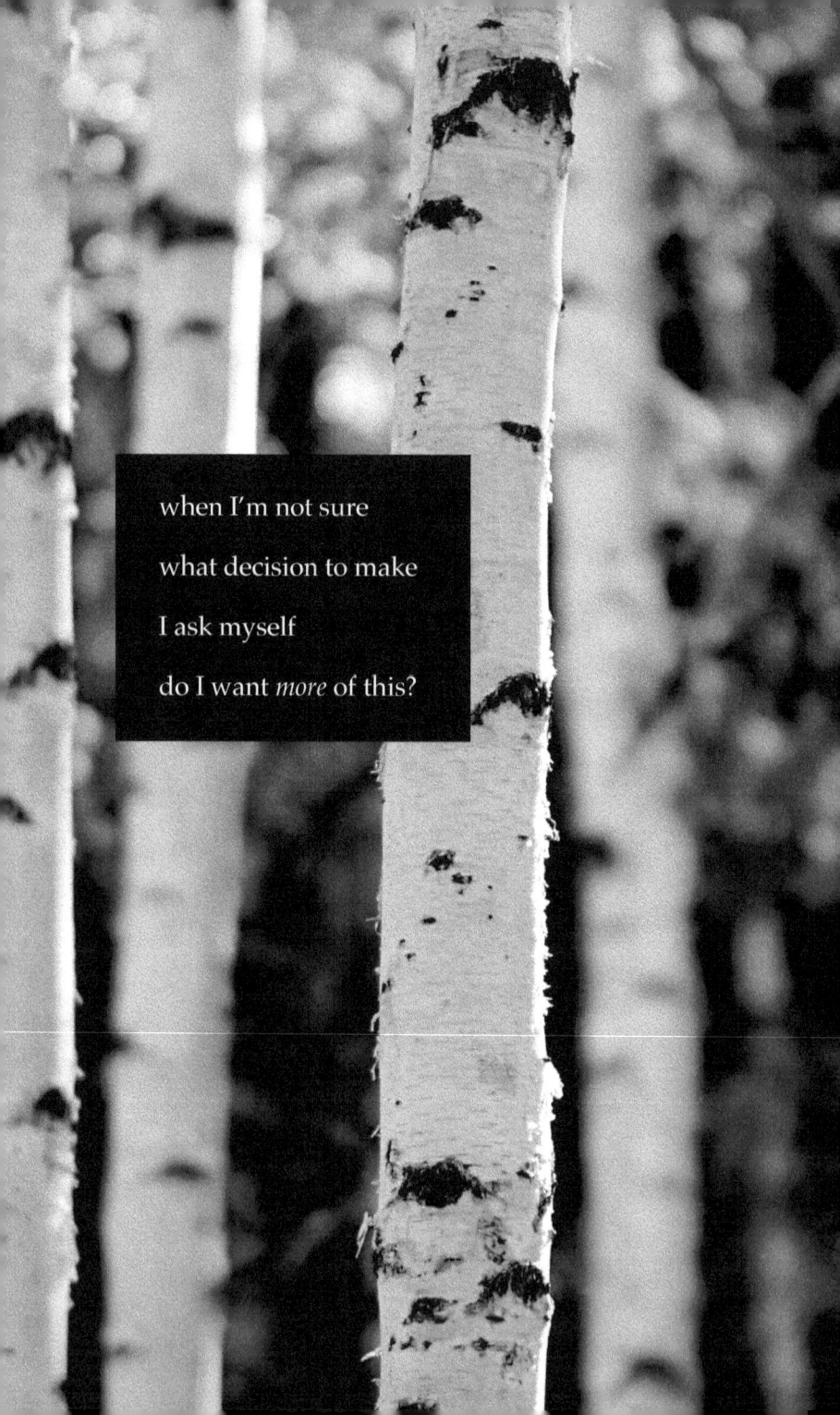

I DISCERN

when I place someone above myself
it's my own soul calling me to rise

I am bigger than these ideas
bigger than these fears
bigger than the things that hold me
and every ounce of me
is worthy

I DISCERN

I will trust myself more of the time

I will not label, define or confine you

to limited ideas sculpted

from the smallest glimpse

into the vastness of your soul

the very nature of life is cyclical
it is contrast and complexity
it is birth and destruction
the flowers that blossom will also rot
they will decompose and return to the earth
but we don't speak about the rotting
and when we don't talk about things
we lose touch with what is real

I DISCERN

let's shine a light

in the places the world tells us

are not worthy of being seen

and free ourselves from

feeling so alone

A Legacy of Love

Mary

I walked into the room and took a deep breath. Mary was lying in the fetal position, fragile and weak, pale and withered. Wild, wiry curls draped over sunken eyes - she looked like she was barely alive. Tears filled my eyes as I noticed the lovingly drawn artwork on the wall; cards to the world's best Nonna, fresh flowers, untouched chocolates and handwritten love notes all around her – evidence of being loved.

The head nurse told me she couldn't understand me and said not to waste my time on Mary because she was long gone. She had been diagnosed with end-stage dementia and was non-responsive for almost a year. I was a second-year nursing student; she was my first patient ever.

When the nurse left, I pulled up a chair and sat beside Mary to introduce myself. It felt a little strange talking, knowing she would never respond, but at the same time, it didn't seem right to be silent. I reached over to touch her hand - it was ice cold. I wrapped her in extra blankets and gently brushed her dark silver hair as I told her about the ruby-red tulips and sweet cherry blossoms in my grandmother's garden. I wondered if she had a garden with flowers in it, too, a couple of pear trees, a grapevine. It seemed like a Nonna thing to talk about.

I tried to feed her, and she clenched her jaw shut. I tried to hold her hands, but they were curled tightly into fists I couldn't open. It felt impossible to care for her: to feed her, bathe her, change her, move her; every detail was a challenge.

I walked into her room each morning, opened the curtains, touched her hand warmly and said, "Good morning, Mary." Naturally, I ignored the advice to just do my job quickly and leave her alone. I became a nurse to heal the world and was naive enough to believe I could. I was determined to give Mary my all, to shower her with compassion, warmth, respect and care. Day after day, I sat at the bottom of the bed and rubbed her feet while telling her stories as though she could understand every word I said.

I DISCERN

After about a week, I tried to feed her again - anticipating her resistance. But, for the first time, she opened her mouth and ate. A few days later, I caught her looking purposefully into my eyes. *She's in there*, I thought. I felt it. I knew it. As I leaned over to help her sit up, she reached for me and firmly grabbed my hand. I stopped everything and looked at her. Tears streamed down her face. This non-responsive woman, this patient not worth wasting time on, was responding - to kindness.

With each passing day, Mary responded more. She began eating well. Her cheeks were rosy; she moved her head and began to regain her strength.

I worked with Mary for 9 weeks. When my rotation on that ward was done, I went to say goodbye. I walked down the corridor to Mary's room, and she wasn't there. My heart sank. I thought she had passed away in the night. I stepped into the sunroom next door and saw her sitting in a chair with her husband and son. Our eyes met, and hers were bright and sparkly.

My heart lit up, and I said, "Good morning, Mary," like I had every morning for weeks.

She looked right at me, smiled and said, "Good morning!"

Her husband began to cry. Her son was shaking, hugging her, and thanking me repeatedly.

End-stage dementia has no cure. It does not reverse. Except that for Mary, it did. The doctor said the diagnosis must have been a mistake.

My inexperience allowed me the openness to access a wisdom that went beyond what can be taught in books or seen in medical reports. Mary taught me to trust myself and showed me that love makes us come alive.

you know the answer

even before you know the question

I DISCERN

I will never dismiss the wisdom of inexperience

there is sacred and immeasurable value

in having nothing yet

to unlearn

I DISCERN

there is a knowing inside of me
that seeks to guide me
I look there
before I look to the world
and after

if you stay

you will disappear

and you are too beautiful

to vanish

before the world has even

had a chance

to breathe you in

I DISCERN

hope was holding me
tethered to a dream
of the man
he would never be
hostage to the life
and the peace
I would never find
until I had the courage
to let my hope in him
die
to my hopes for life

she walked on the earth

as if she belonged to it

not as if she owned it

and together

she and the earth

exhaled

I FOLLOW SOFTNESS

I FOLLOW SOFTNESS

peace is on the horizon
certain like my breath
here now
in and out
even as I sleep
keeping me alive
welcoming me home

she was a galaxy filled with sunsets
woven into an old soul
unscathed by the pain and harshness of the world
and she carried her softness with her everywhere

I FOLLOW SOFTNESS

you belong

right here
in these words
in this life
in the unknowing
in the certainty
in the longing
in the rising
and in between it all

you are enough
you are so enough
that
e n o u g h
can't even contain you

I FOLLOW SOFTNESS

love

ripples through time
like a smooth stone
across the stillness of the lake
on a summers night
it reaches back to mend the hearts
of my grandmothers
and forward to strengthen the softness
of the great, great
grandchildren I will never know
but have already lived lifetimes with

I practiced holding on to nothing
but the knowing that everything will change

she is strong

but she doesn't want to be

she doesn't want to advocate for herself and her sisters

she doesn't want to have to protect her tenderness
from your harsh

she doesn't want to walk in the dark with her hands clenched
for fear of who might harm her

she is strong
but she doesn't want to be

not always
not today

today, she wants to rest

she wants your voice to raise her up
she wants to fall into her softness
and surrender to it
to feel safe and held

just for today

can you be strong
so that she doesn't have to be so strong
all the time

I FOLLOW SOFTNESS

don't tell her she is strong

she knows that

she knows because strong has felt like her only choice

for a long time now

don't tell her she is strong

ask her

how you can help

your tenderness is sacred

and it is needed here

I FOLLOW SOFTNESS

what I heal for myself

I heal for the ancestors

of the past

and

of the future

I am here

to remind you

the space around you and within you

is your home

and it goes with you

everywhere

you belong

today

I will lean in

to the spaciousness

of the unknown

as though

I am cozying up

for a nap

if I had known
the life
and the friendship
and the warmth
and the peace
that was waiting for me
on the other side of my fear
I would have run toward it
with my arms outstretched
instead of tiptoeing away from my old life slowly
over years

I FOLLOW SOFTNESS

I walk between the lines of time
where who I was meets who I am becoming

sometimes a new chapter starts
though I wasn't ready
for the last one to end
and I remember that
like me
life has its own story to tell

I FOLLOW SOFTNESS

softness is strength

a vastly stronger strength

than the strengths that are seen and spoken about

stronger than the strengths

that are valued and praised

in this world

softness is the strength

of water

it can shower you with life

and smooth the sharpest, rockiest edges

rounding corners of compassion

guiding you home

I FOLLOW SOFTNESS

every
tear
was
an
ocean
of
prayers
and
the
universe
heard
you

may exquisite love
be the most familiar
and ordinary experience
of your life

I FOLLOW SOFTNESS

it is a steady-like-your-breath kind of love

constant-like-your-heartbeat love

eternal-like-your-soul love

you-can-rest-in-it love

safe-to-trust-it love

not-going-anywhere love

the love-you-have-for-yourself kind of love

never-settle-for-less

love

the choices

that got me through the hardest seasons of my life

carried me to today

and I love them for that

I FOLLOW SOFTNESS

I hold myself

in the light

of fierce compassion

and love

lay me down
on a warm summer morning
when the sunlit dew meets the air
as roots unfurl
and the grass folds open
to take me into its loving embrace

A JOURNEY OF SOFTENING

To the beat of the drum, I journey to find the truth of who I am. A magnificent oak tree appears before me. With ease, I climb ancient, knotted arms that kiss the clouds. An eagle swoops down to pick me up, and as we soar together, wintry winds whip through my hair.

"I am here to show you yourself," she tells me.

We spiral down towards the earth, riding waves of light to the edge of the forest. We land on a birch tree, and I see my dear friend on a walk.

"This is you," she says.

We turn circles east and fly above the hospital on the day my son was born; peeking in the window, I see him in the incubator, safe and warm.

"This is you," she says.

We soar across the world and meet the glowing mountains as the sun rises in Moorea.

"This is you," she says.

Before I can think, respond or even begin to process any of this, we bolt upward, moving years beyond the earth to perch upon a star. A soft, radiant light fills and surrounds me.

"This is you," she says. I close my eyes, taking it all in.

I open my eyes again and find myself standing in another world, gazing into the grace of the divine.

"I am you," she says.

My heart softens, breath fills my lungs, and peace washes over me. I learn that there is no separation. The universe is my mirror. Everything I see is me. And I am everything I see.

I FOLLOW SOFTNESS

We glide down towards the earth, swirling blissfully, as the eagle brings me back to that beautiful old oak tree. I climb down and feel my bare feet on the cold, silky soil. Everything looks different now. I am filled with greater depths of compassion than I have ever known.

be kind, my heart whispers

as you walk on the earth, you walk on your own heart

as you speak to others, you speak to yourself

I FOLLOW SOFTNESS

she realized her dreams

were E V I D E N C E

of the belief

the universe

had

in

her

and her doubts

turned

into

fire

let the voice of your soul
be louder
than the noise of the world

I FOLLOW SOFTNESS

you, my love,
are the wildest wild
you shake up
the mediocrity
and turn my life inside out
and upside down
and while sometimes
it makes me feel
like I'm in a snow globe
it also reminds me
I am alive

thank you

the desires of your heart
are the beating wisdom
of your soul

A Legacy of Love

♡

Lily

I closed my eyes, said a prayer and knocked at the door. I was always nervous when I knocked for the first time, never quite knowing what was on the other side. I read about my patient's diagnosis and saw the doctor's orders, but I didn't know the things that mattered - not yet.

I crossed the threshold where hope meets acceptance as I entered a room where I did not belong.

She lay in a hospital bed in the middle of the living room - furniture, chairs, plants and decor displaced to make room for a mother - the heart, soul and breath of this home. Curled up in pain, wasting away from her tumultuous journey with cancer and aged decades beyond her 48 years - she seems so small lying there.

My eyes met hers, and I saw them light up. They spoke to me of life, love, courage, faith, and boundless beauty. They wrote the story of a lifetime with no words. She reached her arms out to hold my hand.

"I know it's almost time, but I want to see the snow. I love the snow. I just want to see it one more time," she said in a soft and shaky voice. It was only September.

Lily fought every single day to stay alive, and she was exhausted. Her body was so weak that she could no longer move alone. She depended on her husband and daughter for everything.

I visited her every day, and every day I prayed for snow.

As I sat to write this story, I couldn't remember what kind of cancer she had or what medications she was on. I couldn't remember her husband's name or even where they lived. What I remembered was the glimmer in her eyes, her longing for the snow and her voice – I remembered her voice.

I FOLLOW SOFTNESS

Every day for two weeks, I walked into her home and did my work and as I did, she sang the most beautiful gospel songs. Her voice cracked and trembled - she was in so much pain, but she sang. She sang until she couldn't sing anymore. The day after she stopped singing, I brought her CeCe Winan's album, *Alone in His Presence.* As I played it for her, her tears flowed, and her eyes sparkled.

Lily was holding on. I don't know what was carrying her, if not the arms of pure grace, but she was holding on.

I woke up the next day - the sky was sunny and bright, and the air was fresh, crisp and awakening. On my way to her house, it began to snow. It was the very beginning of October, and it didn't feel cold enough for snow, but it was snowing.

I arrived at her home, and she was outside on the front porch wrapped up in blankets, sitting up with her face stretched up to the sky, feeling the snowflakes kiss her nose and cheeks, smiling a smile I will never forget with her loved ones by her side. She looked at me.

"It's snowing. Celeste, it's snowing!!!"

She waited for it. It came on the sunniest and most beautiful autumn day to greet her and welcome her home. Lily died that afternoon.

Every year, when it snows for the first time, my children jump with delight as they shout for me to wake up and look out the window. I look out, and I think of Lily.

there is love here
and it will carry you
anywhere you need to go

I FOLLOW SOFTNESS

you cannot possibly contain a magic like that

let it spill out of you

let it drip love through the streets

and light through the lives and hearts

of every soul who your soul touches

until the whole world is ablaze

your magic

will remind them

of their own

this is how we heal in community

you can breathe here

beloved

I FOLLOW SOFTNESS

there is a little girl inside of me
and she is promise
she is the sparkle in my eyes
and the skip in my step
she is the love in my heart
and the breath in my body
she believes in magic
and in miracles
she is light
and happy
sincere
and free
and I am here to protect her now

slivers of light reach down through the branches
holding me up
as I talk to the sky
searching its brightness for solace
a single red leaf
taps my shoulder
it says:
let me show you
how to let go

you are not too sensitive
you are paying attention

you are seeing
what the world turns away from

and that
is brave

SENSITIVE SOUL

keep going

I FOLLOW SOFTNESS

she thought about what it would feel like not to TAKE a breath

but to BE it

not to gaze up at the stars

but to blaze as one of them

to be everywhere and nowhere

to weave her essence through the fabric of galaxies

like she was walking from the kitchen to the living room

on a Saturday afternoon

doesn't everyone think about these things?

I AM

rest
and
breath

light
and
peace

shadow
and
heart

promise
and
prayer

I FOLLOW SOFTNESS

I AM

strong
and
soft

open
and
protected

kind
and
fierce

feral
and
free

NOTE TO SELF:

I will do more of what sets my soul on fire

remember
the capacity
you had
before the world filled it up

it
still
belongs
to
you

I have done for today

all that today asks of me

and it is enough

now I will rest

I FOLLOW SOFTNESS

she loved herself how she loved to be loved

the end

I AM GRATEFUL

to the beautiful humans who believed in me from the start and held my book dream safe in their hearts for years
to the ones who have inspired me, mentored me, supported me and encouraged me along the way

I love you

Asha Frost
Christine Marrin
Kristin Harris
Rocky Callen
Marissa Stapley
Chris-Anne Donnelly
Mickey Eves
Sharon Laplante
Nicole Schiener
Iffath Lotallah
Taryn Hawley
Navi Bliss
Adrian Michael Green
David Bedrick
Marjorie Aunos
Sarah Marzalek-Kelly
Adrienne Enns
Rose Candela
Kristen Butler
Anja Simmons
Julie Zepp
Karen Falkenspence

to my loving family
and parents

Breda Woodall
Everett Frenette

to my wonderful children

Jaiden Hsu
Mirahbelle Hsu

www.ingramcontent.com/pod-product-compliance
Lightning Source LLC
Chambersburg PA
CBHW041217130526
44590CB00062BA/4268